Allan and Jean Burgess
Max and Bette Molgard

Bookcraft
Salt Lake City, Utah

ISBN 0-88494-720-3

First Printing, 1989

Printed in the United States of America

NOAH IS OBEDIENT

Genesis 6-8

Noah was a great prophet who lived many years ago. He had three sons who had grown up and were married. Noah was a good father, so he taught his children to do the things that would make Heavenly Father happy. They listened to him and lived righteously.

The rest of the people on the earth listened to their parents also. But because they didn't have good parents, they were being taught things that were wrong. These wicked people were marrying other wicked people and then teaching their children to be wicked.

Heavenly Father could see that the way things were, children could not be taught the right things in the right way. He decided to cleanse the earth so that only Noah and his family would be left. Then all of the children could grow up and teach their children to do right.

Heavenly Father told Noah to make a huge boat called an ark. Noah had never built an ark before, so God told him exactly how to do it. It had to be huge so that Noah could take a male and a female of each of the birds and animals. The birds and animals would be safe in the ark and, when the flood was over, they could have baby animals and birds.

Noah did just as he was told even though he didn't live by a big lake or an ocean. He lived on dry land, so that is where he built the ark. People probably made fun of him for building such a big boat on dry land, but Noah didn't care—he was doing what Heavenly Father wanted him to do.

Then Noah went onto the ark with his family and all of the birds and animals that God had chosen to be saved. It started to rain—not just a sprinkle, but a hard rain. And it kept on raining and raining. It rained until the whole earth was covered with water. Even the tallest mountains were covered. The ark floated and floated. Noah and his family were in the ark over one full year before the ark finally landed on dry ground. They let the animals and birds go and thanked Heavenly Father that their lives had been saved. Noah and his family were the only people left in the world.

It was hard for Noah to do what Heavenly Father asked him to do. Other people, maybe even some of his friends, may have made fun of him and laughed at him. Sometimes we are laughed at for doing what is right. If this happens to us we can remember Noah. Heavenly Father blessed Noah for doing what is right, and we will be blessed when we do what is right.

Cross out the names of the animals in the circles below. There will be five words left. Write these five words in the correct order in the blanks below to finish the sentence and learn something about Noah.

________ WAS __________ BUT __________ DID __________ WAS __________ .

Color in each area that has exactly three sides, and you'll see something that Noah took on the ark.

ABRAHAM THINKS OF OTHERS

Genesis 11–14

Abraham was a great prophet. He had a brother named Haran. When his brother died, Abraham told Haran's son, Lot, that he could live with him. Abraham treated Lot like his own son. He taught him how to do many things. They worked hard together for many years. They both became very rich and had many cattle, sheep, and goats. In fact, they had so many animals that there was not enough grass on the land where they were kept for all of the animals to eat.

Abraham and Lot had servants that took care of their animals for them. Soon these servants were fighting among each other because they all wanted their animals to have the best grass. The animals simply needed more room.

Abraham didn't want any fighting. He told Lot to choose which land he wanted for his animals, and Abraham was willing to take the land that was left. He told Lot that he could choose first. After everything Abraham had done for Lot, Lot should have let Abraham choose first. But Lot was selfish and seemed to think only of himself. He looked at the nice green land that was near the wicked city of Sodom and chose it for himself. He gave Abraham the land that he thought was second best.

Soon after Lot took his animals to the grassy land, an army came to fight the city of Sodom. This army took all of Lot's animals and riches and made Lot and his family go back with them as prisoners. When Abraham heard what had happened, he could have thought that Lot got what he deserved for being selfish. But he didn't! Instead, Abraham thought first of Lot's needs. He loved Lot and wanted to help him.

Abraham asked his men to go with him, and they fought and defeated the army that had captured Lot. They recovered all of Lot's animals and riches, and, best of all, Lot and his family were saved.

Many times each day we make choices. Many of these choices will be whether we should think first of others or whether we should think first of ourselves. Should we share a toy? Should we be kind to others? Should we help when we are asked to?

Heavenly Father and Jesus would like us to choose to be unselfish and think of others first. When we make other people happy, we make ourselves and Heavenly Father happy also.

In the three columns below you will find ten words that have been mixed up. The first part of each word is in column A, the second part in column B, and the last part in column C. These ten words go in the blanks of the ten statements from the story. Figure out each word and write it in the correct blank. (Hint: The word prophet *has been circled so you can see how the columns work.)*

A	B	C
PRO	SON	TS
DE	IM	ET
FIG	RA	ED
CH	HER	ING
PRI	PH	FISH
UN	O	HAM
AN	HT	ALS
OT	FEAT	S
AB	VAN	ICES
SER	SEL	ERS

1. Abraham was a great _________________ .

2. There were too many _________________ and not enough grass.

3. The _________________ were fighting with each other.

4. Abraham didn't want any _________________ .

5. Lot and his family were taken as _________________ .

6. _________________ thought first about Lot's needs.

7. Abraham _________________ the army that had captured Lot.

8. Every day we make many _________________ .

9. We should be kind to _________________ .

10. Heavenly Father wants us to be _________________ .

__________ __________ and __________ would like us to

__________ to be __________ and __________

of __________ __________ .

JOSEPH FORGIVES

Genesis 37–47

Joseph had ten older brothers. Because Joseph was more righteous than his brothers, he was promised the birthright blessing. This meant that he would become the family leader when their father, who was named Jacob, died.

Joseph's brothers didn't think it was fair that their younger brother was going to be over them. All of the brothers were jealous of Joseph.

Once, all of the older brothers were miles away taking care of their father's sheep. Jacob asked Joseph if he would go find his brothers and see if everything was all right. Even though it would take three days to get to where his brothers were, Joseph was glad to do it for his father.

When the brothers saw him coming, they decided to kill him. Anger can open the door for Satan to tempt us to do things we would never do if we were not angry. That is exactly what happened to Joseph's brothers. They tied Joseph up and threw him into a deep pit. Then they saw some rich merchants passing by on their way to Egypt. They decided to sell Joseph to the merchants. This way they would never have to see Joseph again and they would not have to kill him to get rid of him.

When we do things that are wrong, we often think we have to do more wrong things to cover up what we have done. This is what the brothers did. They didn't want to tell their father what they had done, so they killed a small goat and rubbed Joseph's coat in the goat's blood. Then they lied to Jacob and told him that Joseph had been killed and that the blood on his coat was Joseph's own blood.

As a slave in Egypt Joseph continued to do what God wanted him to do. Because of this he was blessed; finally, he was put in charge of all of Egypt and was next in command to the Pharaoh of Egypt.

There was a famine in Israel where Jacob's family lived and they had no food. Jacob heard that there was grain in Egypt so he sent his ten older sons to Egypt to try to buy some. When they arrived in Egypt they were sent to see Joseph, who was over all of the grain. Because it had been so many years, they didn't recognize Joseph, but he recognized them.

As Joseph listened to them and asked them questions, he found that he had a younger brother named Benjamin. Joseph wondered if his brothers had changed since they had sold him into Egypt, so he tested them by asking them to do many things. When he found that his brothers would give up their own lives to protect Benjamin, he realized they had changed. He told them who he was and cried tears of joy because he was finally with his family again. Joseph could have been angry with his brothers for what they had done to him, but instead he forgave them. He sent his brothers to get his father, and they all came back to Egypt and lived with Joseph.

Feelings of love and forgiveness help us listen to Heavenly Father. Sometimes when we are angry or jealous, we can sing a favorite song to help us replace these feelings. When someone does something to hurt us, we can love them and forgive them just as Joseph did with his brothers. Then Heavenly Father will be happy, and we will be much happier also.

Write the words that match the clues into the circles below. The first letter of each word has been written in. Finish each word by writing the rest of the letters in the circles that are connected with lines. Then write the correct word next to each clue. (Hint: The word that matches the first clue is Egypt.)

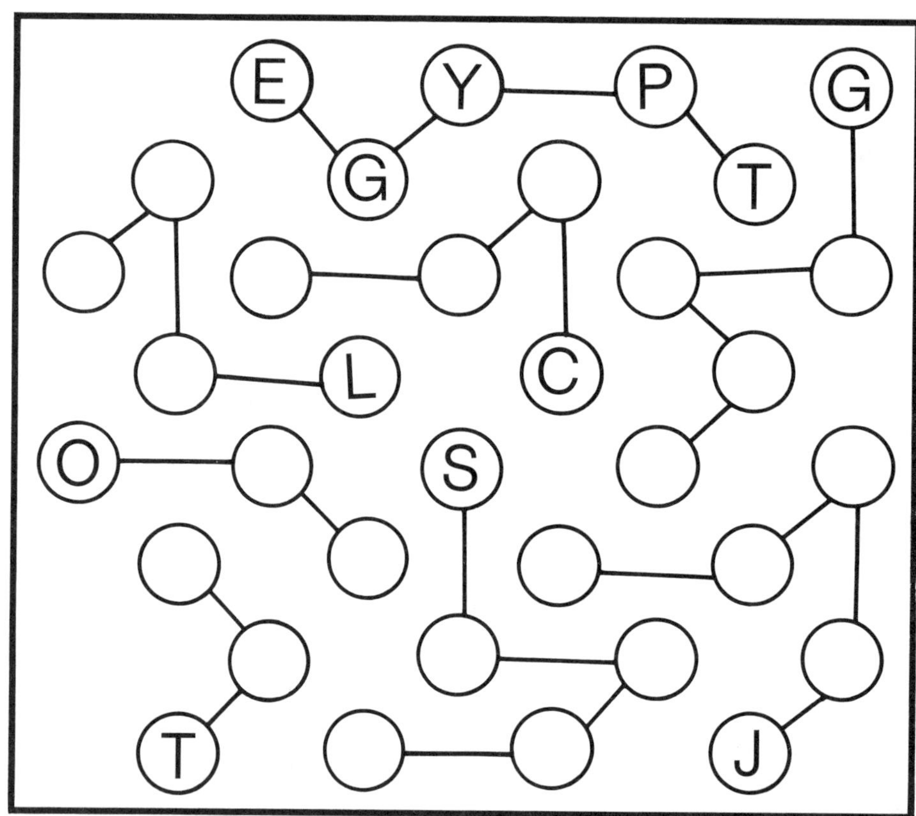

ANSWERS   CLUES

— — — — —	1. Place where Joseph became leader.
— — — — —	2. What the brothers wanted to buy.
— — — —	3. What the brothers put blood on.
— — — — —	4. The name of Joseph's father.
— — — — — —	5. The person who wants us to get angry.
— — —	6. The number of older brothers Joseph had.
— — —	7. The number of younger brothers Joseph had.
— — — —	8. The feeling that brings happiness.

Hidden below are the missing words to complete the names of songs that you could sing to help you feel better when you get mad at someone.

```
J   K   G   M   O   R   M   O   N   L   N   S   P   N   V
Y   G   O   L   D   E   N   G   A   S   S   A   W   J   N
N   M   O   E   R   G   G   D   R   K   I   X   G   O   E
C   A   M   C   B   V   S   A   I   D   V   N   X   P   H
G   D   A   I   A   O   S   Q   G   F   D   P   K   F   O
G   C   H   I   L   D   O   U   A   P   J   O   V   N   V
L   E   V   Y   I   D   D   K   N   E   I   D   F   F   E
F   H   D   N   S   S   N   W   L   B   X   I   Y   A   S
U   S   I   K   O   Y   E   T   E   G   E   O   V   V   H
T   M   U   J   Z   S   T   E   X   X   B   A   K   N   I
R   Q   K   G   T   I   U   N   L   Z   H   R   M   C   O
B   W   C   N   L   D   W   X   J   E   S   U   S   H   O
V   A   A   N   D   G   B   X   K   Q   E   G   U   K   W
K   W   B   U   O   O   E   Z   S   E   N   H   O   O   H
U   W   V   S   Z   R   R   K   W   V   D   D   L   D   D
```

Give, _______________ the _______________ Stream

_______________ of _______________ Stories

_______________ _______________ Me for a _______________

I _______________ a _______________ of _______________

The _______________ Plates

DAVID FIGHTS GOLIATH

I Samuel 17

A man named Jesse had seven sons. His youngest son was named David. David's job was to watch his father's sheep. Watching sheep might sound like an easy job, but it wasn't. David had to make sure the sheep didn't wander away. If they did, they could get lost. There were even wild animals in that country that liked to eat sheep; David had killed a lion and a bear protecting his father's sheep. He didn't have a gun. He just had a sling shot. It was a long, thin leather rope with a pocket tied in the middle. David would put a rock in the pocket and hold both ends of the rope. Then he would whip it around and around over his head until it was spinning very fast. David would then let go of one end of the rope and the rock would whiz out of the pocket so fast that it could kill even large animals. David practiced and practiced until he could make the rock go anyplace he wanted it to go.

One day while David was watching the sheep, his father, Jesse, came to him and asked him if he would go and find out how his older brothers were doing. They were several miles away fighting for the army of Israel. They were fighting the Philistines. In Bible times there were no telephones or radios or televisions to use to find out what was happening far away, so David was sent to see for himself.

When David found his brothers, he saw that they were afraid. So was everyone else in the Israelite army. They were afraid of a Philistine giant named Goliath.

David's frightened brothers said that Goliath had been yelling at them for forty days. He wanted one man from their army to fight against him. Goliath said if they killed him, the Philistines would be the Israelites' slaves. If Goliath won, the Israelites would become the Philistines' slaves. Goliath felt that he was so big and strong that he could beat anyone. He made fun of the Israelites because no one dared to fight him. He also made fun of their God.

David's brothers told him that he had better go back and watch the sheep, but David said that he was going to fight the giant. He said that if he had Heavenly Father to help him fight, no one could beat him—not even a giant.

The king told David to use the king's own protective armor, but David had never fought with armor before so he didn't use it. David said a prayer, picked up five smooth stones for his sling shot, and went out to fight Goliath.

When Goliath saw David he laughed and said, "You, a boy, think you can fight me?"

David told him he was fighting with the help of his God. He took a stone, placed it in his sling shot, and sent it whizzing toward Goliath. The stone hit Goliath on the forehead and the giant fell to the earth. Then David rushed forward and cut off Goliath's head with his own sword.

Many times in our lives it seems like we are fighting a giant. The giant might be friends who want us to do something wrong or it may be a test at school or even getting along with others. We all have giants in our lives. But if we pray and have faith that Heavenly Father will help us, he'll help us fight our giants just as he did with David.

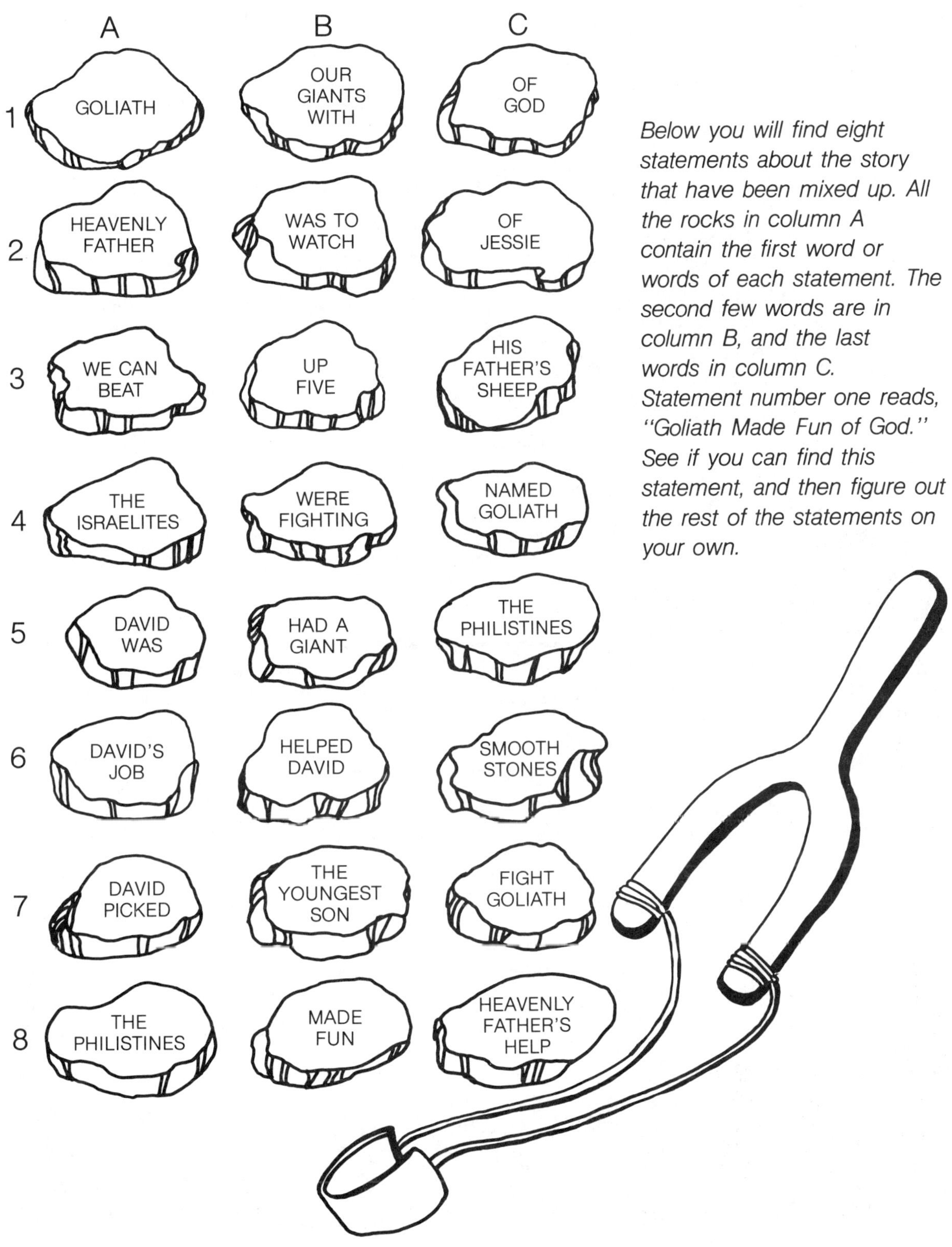

Below you will find eight statements about the story that have been mixed up. All the rocks in column A contain the first word or words of each statement. The second few words are in column B, and the last words in column C. Statement number one reads, "Goliath Made Fun of God." See if you can find this statement, and then figure out the rest of the statements on your own.

Using the clues below, write in the six things that can help you overcome giants in your life!

You lived with Him in heaven.
He is the father of your ward.
The people who live in the same house with you.
They are your age and you play with them.
They teach you the gospel.
You should read them every day.

G __ __
__ I __ __ __ __
__ A __ __ __ __
__ __ __ __ N __ __
T __ __ __ __ __ __ __
S __ __ __ __ __ __ __

JONATHAN — A TRUE FRIEND

I Samuel 18-23

After David killed Goliath, he went to live with King Saul, who had a son named Jonathan. David and Jonathan spent a lot of time together and became good friends. Jonathan grew to love David the same as if David had been his brother, and David loved Jonathan the same way.

At first, Saul loved David too, but David was so good at everything that Saul started to worry that people would think David was better than he was. Saul came up with a plan to get rid of David.

One of the prizes Saul had promised to the person who dared to fight Goliath was that he would get to marry one of his daughters. Saul told David he could marry his daughter only if he killed one hundred more Philistines. Saul thought that David would be killed himself before he could kill a hundred Philistines. But David wasn't. He killed more than a hundred and came back to marry Saul's daughter.

Saul's plan had backfired. Now all of the Israelites knew David was a wonderful warrior—he was their hero. Saul was jealous and furious. He decided to make sure David would be killed.

Jonathan could have been jealous. He knew that David was going to be the next king even though the king's son usually became king. But he didn't think about himself. He just thought about his friend David. He was proud of all that David had done and knew that David would need his help if he was going to be kept safe from his father Saul. Jonathan warned David and told him to hide. He said that he would find out if it was safe to come back to the king's palace. When he found out that Saul still wanted David killed, he ran and warned David again.

David had to hide from Saul for many years. During this time, Jonathan helped Saul fight many battles and tried to be a good and obedient son, except when Saul would try to hurt his friend David. Jonathan knew his father was doing something wrong, so he did everything he could do to make sure David was safe. Jonathan's life was in danger several times, but he still chose to protect his friend David.

Friendships are important. The best way to have a good friend is to be a good friend. Friends aren't just for doing fun things with, but good friends always think about each other. They make choices that will help their friends to be happy. They listen when their friends need help and they watch out for their friends. If they see them doing something wrong or someone else doing something to hurt them, they do everything they can to help their friends. That's what Jonathan did for David. They were true friends.

The eight words in the circle below all end with the same letter. Figure out what the letter is and then use the words to fill in the blanks in the sentences.

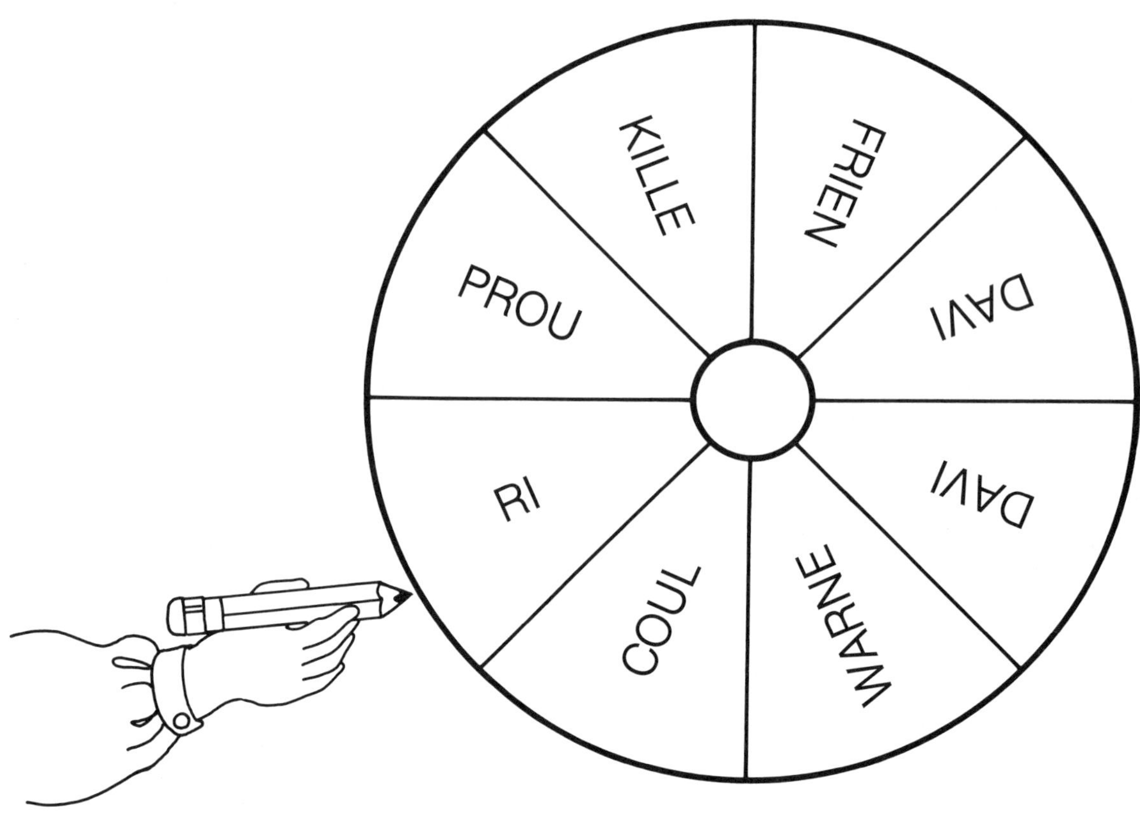

1. _________________ went to live with King Saul.

2. Saul's son, Jonathan, was David's _____________________ .

3. Saul tried to get ____________ of David.

4. _________________ became a hero to the Israelites.

5. Jonathan ________________ have been jealous but he wasn't.

6. Jonathan was ________________ of David.

7. Jonathan ________________ David and told him to hide.

8. David had to hide from Saul for many years so that he would not

   be ____________________ .

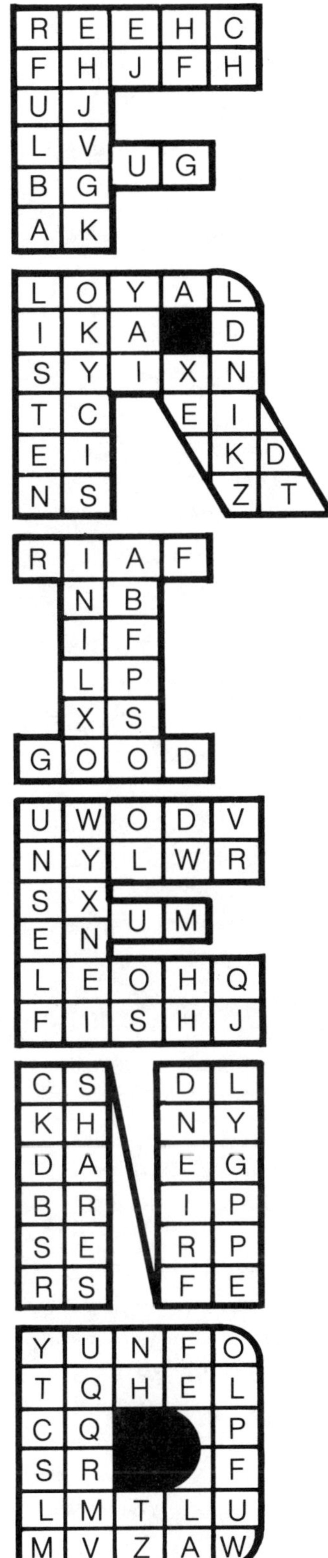

*In the letters
of the word
FRIEND there
are ten hidden
words that have
to do with being
a friend.*

These words go—

- *up and down,*
- *forward and backward,*
- *and even around corners.*

*See if you can find
all ten of them!*

NAAMAN IS HEALED
II Kings 5

Naaman was the commander of the king's army in Syria. He had helped the king win many battles, but now he was very sick.

In Bible days there was a terrible skin disease that people were afraid of getting. It was called leprosy, and there was no medicine that would help it. People with leprosy would get big sores all over their bodies. These sores would never heal but would keep getting bigger and bigger until the person would die. Naaman had leprosy.

A small girl who was a servant to Naaman's wife told her about Elisha. Elisha was a prophet in Israel. Doctors couldn't cure leprosy but a prophet could.

Naaman went to Israel to find Elisha. As soon as he got to Elisha's home, Elisha told a servant to tell Naaman to wash himself seven times in the Jordan River and he would be cured. Naaman should have been happy, but he wasn't. He was mad. He had expected a beautiful blessing or a miraculous healing under the touch of a prophet's hand, not to be told by a servant to go take seven baths in a muddy river. He did not even get to see Elisha the prophet. He left Elisha's home very angry.

His servants told him he should at least try it. After all, he had come a long way and he just might be cured of leprosy. He went to the Jordan River and bathed himself seven times. At the end of the seventh time, his sores disappeared and his skin became as smooth and beautiful as a little child's.

Naaman had left Syria with rich and wonderful gifts for the person that would cure him. He took the presents and money to pay Elisha for healing him. Elisha told him that he hadn't healed him. He taught him that the power that had healed him had been given to him by God. He said that he could not accept any gifts for using the priesthood. Naaman thanked him and started home.

One of Elisha's servants named Gehazi had seen all of the money and gifts. He couldn't understand why Elisha didn't take them and couldn't get them out of his mind. Finally he couldn't stand it any longer. He wanted them for himself!

He ran after Naaman and told him that Elisha had decided he wanted some of the money. Naaman gladly gave it to him. When Gehazi returned, Elisha asked him where he had been. He lied again and said he hadn't been anywhere. Elisha knew Gehazi was lying. He said that as a punishment for his selfishness and dishonesty he would have Naaman's leprosy.

It would be easy to always be honest if we got sick every time we told a lie. But it doesn't happen exactly that way. Our bodies don't usually get sick, but our spirits do. Every lie we tell makes our spirit a little bit weaker; like Gehazi's first lie, one lie always leads to more lies. Pretty soon people don't trust us anymore.

The best way to keep our spirit healthy is to always do things that we won't have to lie about. We will be happier and others around us will trust us more if we always tell the truth.

To the right is a secret code key. Every letter in the key is identified by two numbers—a horizontal and a vertical one. For example: 16 = A; 27 = G; 37-110-28-29 = LEHI. Using the secret code key, decode the following words and match them with the correct questions.

*	6	7	8	9	10
1	A	B	C	D	E
2	F	G	H	I	J
3	K	L	M	N	O
4	P	Q	R	S	T
5	U	V	W	Y	Z

___ 1. Naaman was the ________________ of the King's army.

___ 2. Naaman had a disease called ________________ .

___ 3. Naaman went to ________________ to be healed.

___ 4. Elisha told a servant to have Naaman wash seven times in the ________ River.

___ 5. Naaman's skin became ________________ and beautiful like a child's.

___ 6. Elisha wouldn't accept Naaman's ________________ .

___ 7. The servant named ________________ wanted the gifts for himself.

___ 8. Gehazi ________________ to Elisha.

___ 9. Gehazi's punishment for being ________________ was leprosy.

___10. We will be ________________ if we always tell the truth.

A. $\overline{49}$ $\overline{38}$ $\overline{310}$ $\overline{310}$ $\overline{410}$ $\overline{28}$

B. $\overline{28}$ $\overline{16}$ $\overline{46}$ $\overline{46}$ $\overline{29}$ $\overline{110}$ $\overline{48}$

C. $\overline{27}$ $\overline{110}$ $\overline{28}$ $\overline{16}$ $\overline{510}$ $\overline{29}$

D. $\overline{18}$ $\overline{310}$ $\overline{38}$ $\overline{38}$ $\overline{16}$ $\overline{39}$ $\overline{19}$ $\overline{110}$ $\overline{48}$

E. $\overline{110}$ $\overline{37}$ $\overline{29}$ $\overline{49}$ $\overline{28}$ $\overline{16}$

F. $\overline{19}$ $\overline{29}$ $\overline{49}$ $\overline{28}$ $\overline{310}$ $\overline{39}$ $\overline{110}$ $\overline{49}$ $\overline{410}$

G. $\overline{27}$ $\overline{29}$ $\overline{26}$ $\overline{410}$ $\overline{49}$

H. $\overline{37}$ $\overline{110}$ $\overline{46}$ $\overline{48}$ $\overline{310}$ $\overline{49}$ $\overline{59}$

I. $\overline{210}$ $\overline{310}$ $\overline{48}$ $\overline{19}$ $\overline{16}$ $\overline{39}$

J. $\overline{37}$ $\overline{29}$ $\overline{110}$ $\overline{19}$

In the maze below you may travel one box at a time up, down, left, or right, but not diagonally. You may only move between boxes if the words in those boxes can be joined in a sentence that gives you an important message. The first three words are "THE MORE YOU." Using these rules, can you find your way from the boy to the spider?

THE	STOP	GO	JOB	DOES	SISTER	DOOR	LEG
MORE	YOU	LIE	SET	IS	TO	REMEM-BER	WHAT
OUT	OFF	THE	HARDER	IT	UP	CAT	YOU
LINE	SPACE	CAR	HOUSE	DOG	UNTIL	SAID	HAVE
BOY	DESK	TABLE	SPOON	CAKE	YOU	GET	FROG
SPIDER	WOOD	CAGE	BALL	OVER	IN	CAUGHT	FINGER
WATER	PEN	HAT	HORSE	MAZE	A	COW	TOE
PAPER	BAT	RED	WALK	OF	YOUR	OWN	LIES

JONAH

Jonah 1–3

The capital city of Assyria was Nineveh. It was a big city full of many people. These people had never had a prophet. They had never been taught about Heavenly Father so they prayed to statues. They had never been taught the commandments so they didn't know how to live in order to be worthy to live with God someday.

Heavenly Father decided to send a prophet to teach the gospel to the people of Nineveh. He spoke to a prophet in Israel named Jonah and asked him to go and teach the people of Nineveh.

Jonah knew about the wickedness of Nineveh. They were so cruel and wicked that everyone had heard about them. The very last place Jonah wanted to serve a mission was Nineveh. So he did a very foolish thing. He tried to hide from God. He got in a boat and tried to run away.

Nobody can run away from Heavenly Father. He sent a huge storm that rocked Jonah's boat back and forth. The storm got worse and worse until it looked like the boat was going to break into pieces. The other men on the boat decided God must be mad at someone in the boat. They decided to draw straws to see whom God was angry with. Jonah got the shortest straw. He told them that their assumption was true and that he was a prophet trying to run away from the Lord.

Jonah told them to throw him overboard and their lives would be saved. As soon as they did this the storm stopped. Then, before Jonah could drown, Heavenly Father sent a big fish to swallow him.

Jonah was caught alive in the belly of a big fish. There's not much to do in the belly of a fish except think, and that's what Jonah did. He thought of how he'd been wrong to hide from God and how he'd make a better decision if he was given another chance. Heavenly Father knew what Jonah was thinking so he made the fish swim to land and throw Jonah up. Then he asked Jonah again to go to Nineveh. This time Jonah went. He taught the people and the whole city listened, repented, and became good people.

Heavenly Father probably won't send a fish to swallow us up when we're not doing what he's asked us to do, but he has given us the Holy Ghost. When we do something wrong, the Holy Ghost will make us feel mixed up or bad.

But if we do right things, the Holy Ghost will make us feel good inside. As we listen to the Holy Ghost, we will know what to do.

In this crossword puzzle, the clues appear inside the grid. Fill in the answers in the direction of the arrows.

Use the secret code below to find out something that Jonah might have been thinking while he was in the belly of the fish.

DANIEL PRAYS
Daniel 6

Persia had become a huge country by defeating many other countries and making them part of Persia. A man named Darius was the king over all of Persia. Persia was so large that Darius had chosen 120 men to help him rule over the people. He had chosen other men to rule over the 120 men.

A man named Daniel was chosen to rule over everyone but the king. He was an Israelite and had been taken captive when the city of Jerusalem had been defeated. Because of his great faith, God had helped Daniel and he had become very wise. King Darius recognized that the Spirit of the Lord was with Daniel and he respected and loved him very much. The other rulers were jealous of Daniel and wanted to get rid of him, but they couldn't find anything he did that was wrong.

Finally the rulers came up with a plan. They knew how much Daniel loved God and that he prayed three times a day. They decided to write a new law that said no one could pray to anyone but Darius for thirty days. They knew that Daniel loved God too much to stop praying. The law said that anyone who prayed to someone else during the thirty days would be thrown into a den of lions.

They took the new law to King Darius and convinced him that it was a good law. When he signed the law he was not thinking about Daniel and how he prayed three times a day. In those days, when a king signed a law, it could not be changed even if the king wanted it changed.

It wasn't long before Daniel heard about the law. He knelt down to pray right in front of his window where everyone could see him. The men grabbed him and took him to the king. They told the king that Daniel needed to be thrown into the lions' den.

The king was very upset because he loved Daniel and knew that he could not change the law. He told Daniel that he hoped that God would save him. The man then threw Daniel into the lions' den and rolled a huge stone in front of it so Daniel couldn't get out.

King Darius didn't eat or sleep that night but fasted all night for his friend Daniel. Early the next morning the king hurried to the lions' den and called out to Daniel, "Did your God save you?"

Daniel called back, "Yes! He sent an angel to shut the lions' mouths, and they have not hurt me!"

Darius was so happy that his friend had not been hurt that he made a law that all people should respect Daniel's God.

We don't have laws that tell us not to pray, but Satan tries to get us not to. He tells us that we are too tired or that it is all right to miss just one night. He knows how important prayer really is.

Heavenly Father tells us that he wants to hear from us every morning and every night. We might want to tell him each morning what we are going to do that day. We can tell him what we are thankful for and what we need extra help with. Then, each night we can tell him how we did that day.

Any time that we need his help during the day, we can pray and ask him for it. If we are where we can't kneel down, we can even pray quietly in our hearts and he will hear us.

It is such a blessing to be able to pray and talk to Heavenly Father whenever we want to or need to. Daniel knew how important prayer was and Heavenly Father blessed him. As you pray, Heavenly Father will bless you also.

In the round maze there are eight different ways to escape from the lions' den. Write the correct word in the first statement. Then, starting in the lions' den, and using the letters of the word, find your way out of the den. Do the same with each statement until you have escaped eight different ways.

1. Darius was the king of __ __ __ __ __ __ .

2. God helped __ __ __ __ __ __ become very wise.

3. King Darius recognized the __ __ __ __ __ __ of the Lord.

4. King __ __ __ __ __ __ loved Daniel very much.

5. The other __ __ __ __ __ __ were jealous of Daniel.

6. Daniel __ __ __ __ __ __ three times a day.

7. A huge stone was __ __ __ __ __ __ in front of the lions' den.

8. God sent an angel to shut the lions' __ __ __ __ __ __ .

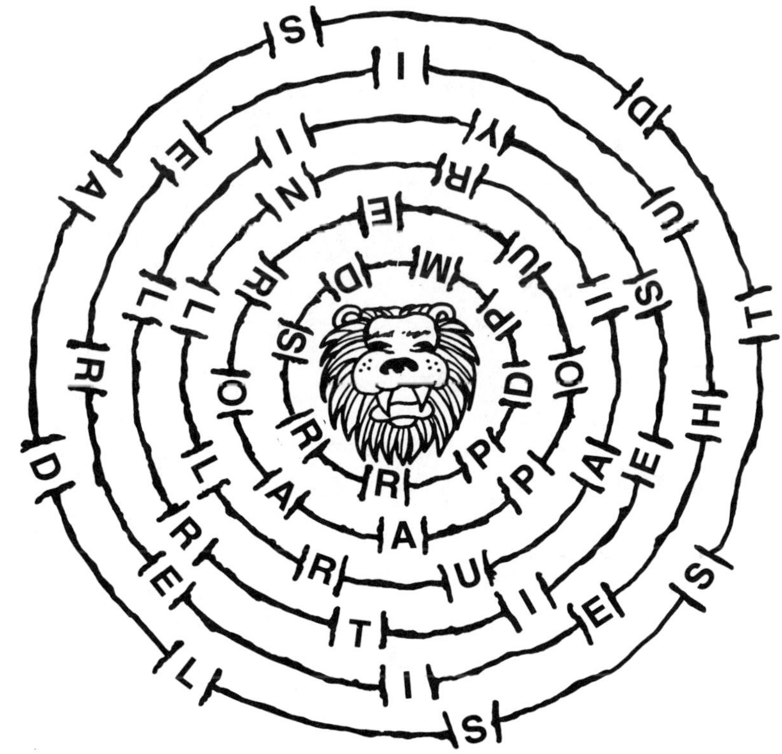

Circle the word in each square that does not belong with the other words. Then write the circled words in the blanks below to discover what the message is.

STAND WALK RUN PRAY 1	NIGHT MOON STARS MORNING 2	NIGHT SUN LIGHT MORNING 3
DOG HEAVENLY CAT MOUSE 4	FIREMAN FATHER POLICEMAN DOG CATCHER 5	LOOK HEAR SEE PEEK 6
BLESS YELL CURSE SWEAR 7	WHEELS YOU ENGINE HORN 8	WAGON SCOOTER LOVES BIKE 9

If you will ____________ ____________ and
           1   2

____________, ____________ ____________
   3   4   5

will ____________ you and ____________
      6   7

____________ because he ____________ you.
   8   9

ESTHER SAVES
HER PEOPLE

Esther 1–7

The king of Persia had divorced his wife and was looking for a new one. He decided that all of the beautiful girls from all the cities in Persia should parade in front of him and he would choose the prettiest one. He chose a girl named Esther.

Esther's uncle was named Mordecai. They both had an ancestor named Judah. So did their family of aunts, uncles, and cousins. Because this big family of hundreds of people were all part of Judah's family, they were called Jews. Not everyone liked Jews, so Mordecai told Esther to keep it a secret that she was a Jew.

Many times Mordecai sat at the gate of the king's palace. One day he heard that two of the king's men were going to kill the king. He told Esther, who told the king, and the men were put to death. As a reward, Mordecai's name was put in an important record kept by the king.

A man named Haman acted like he was a friend of the king. The king liked Haman so much that he made him a leader over the other leaders.

Haman loved the power this gave him. He thought he was better than everyone else and wanted everyone to bow down to him whenever he passed by them.

One day when Haman passed by Mordecai, Mordecai not only wouldn't bow down to Haman but also wouldn't even get out of his chair. Haman was furious. He found out that Mordecai was a Jew and decided that not only would he have Mordecai killed but also all of the other Jews.

He convinced the king that all the Jews should be killed because they would not bow down to anyone but their God. The king signed a law that all of the Jews would be killed on a certain day. When Mordecai heard about the law, he ran to tell Esther. He knew she was their only hope.

Esther told Mordecai to ask all of the Jews to fast and pray for three days. She would then talk to the king and let him know she was a Jew.

This would not be just a regular wife-to-husband talk. The king had many strange rules. One of them was that if people came to talk to him without him sending for them first, he could have them killed. Esther would be risking her life to talk to the king. But Esther loved her family and the other Jewish people.

After three days of fasting and prayer, she made herself look beautiful and went into the king. The king saw how beautiful she was and decided not to have her killed. He told her he would give her anything she wanted. She asked the king to invite Haman to dinner and said that she would tell him what she wanted at dinner.

Haman decided the king must like him very much to invite him to dinner, so he planned on asking the king for permission to hang Mordecai.

At the dinner the king asked Esther what she wanted most. She told him she was a Jew and that the people that were to be killed were her family and friends. She also reminded the king that Mordecai had once saved the king's life. When the king found out that Haman was planning on killing Mordecai, he had Haman put to death instead. Esther's people were all saved.

Esther must have been scared when she stood up for her family. But she knew that families are one of the most important gifts that Heavenly Father has given us. Family members are always ready to help us when we need it. We need to be ready to help our family at all times, because our family is one of the few things that can last forever—that is, it can if we take care of it properly.

Fill in the missing letters in the statements below. You will find out something very important by using the numbers below the letters to fill in the secret message wheel.

1. The king of Persia wanted __sther to be his wi__e.
    19   1

2. Esther's uncle was n__med __ordecai.
    2   3

3. Members of Esther's fam__ly were ca__led Jews.
    4   5

4. Haman thought he was b__tter than e__eryone el__e.
    7   18   8

5. Hama__ __onvinced the king that all Jews should __e killed.
    11   9   12

6. __sther risked her life for he__ __amily.
    13   16   14

7. Esther s__ved all of her p__ople.
    10   17

8. We sh__uld be __eady to help our famil__es at all times.
    15   20   6

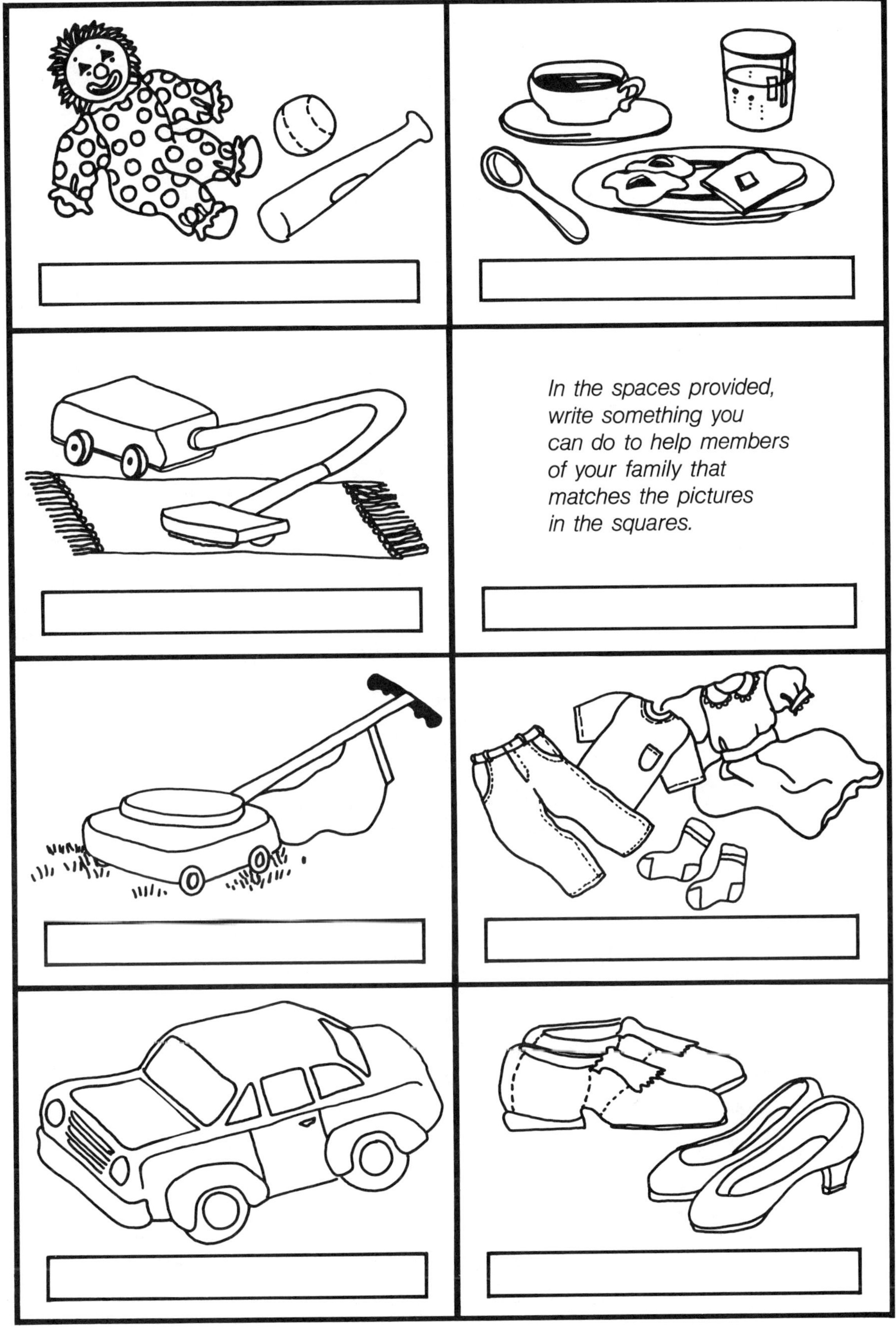
In the spaces provided,
write something you
can do to help members
of your family that
matches the pictures
in the squares.